GREAT ICE BEAR

THE POLAR BEAR AND THE ESKIMO

DOROTHY HINSHAW PATENT

ILLUSTRATED BY ANNE WERTHEIM

MORROW JUNIOR BOOKS

NEW YORK

The author wishes to thank
Charles Jonkel, Ph.D., Director,
Ursid Research Center, and David
Rockwell, author of *Giving Voice to
Bear,* for reading and commenting
on this manuscript.

Acrylic paints were used for the full-color illustrations.
The text type is 13-point Galliard.

Published by Morrow Junior Books
a division of William Morrow and Company, Inc.
1350 Avenue of the Americas, New York, NY 10019
www.williammorrow.com

Printed in Singapore at Tien Wah Press.

1 2 3 4 5 6 7 8 9 10

Library of Congress Cataloging-in-Publication Data
Patent, Dorothy Hinshaw.
Great ice bear: the polar bear and the eskimo / Dorothy Hinshaw Patent;
illustrated by Anne Wertheim.
p. cm.
Includes index.
Summary: Gives information about polar bears, which inhabit the
arctic regions of Russia, Norway, Canada, the United States, Denmark,
and Greenland, and discusses their relationships with humans.
ISBN 0-688-13767-9 (trade)—ISBN 0-688-13768-7 (library)
1. Polar bear—Juvenile literature. [1. Polar bear. 2. Bears.
3. Human-animal relationships.] I. Wertheim, Anne, ill. II. Title.
QL737.C27P3626 1999 599.786—dc21 97-44820 CIP AC

To Charles Jonkel,
one of the polar bear's
best friends
D.H.P.

To my loving family
from Hamburg to Haiku,
and especially to Shali
A.W.

CONTENTS

This map shows where polar bears live in the region surrounding the North Pole.

RUSSIA

ARCTIC CIRCLE

SIBERIA

KARA SEA

RUSSIA

LAPTEV SEA

Murmansk

FINLAND

BARENTS SEA

ARCTIC OCEAN

Hammerfest

NORTH POLE
+

NORWAY
SWEDEN

SPITSBERGEN

CHUKCHI SEA

ICELAND

Barrow

GREENLAND
(Denmark)

ALASKA (USA)

Thule

BEAUFORT SEA

BAFFIN BAY

ARCTIC CIRCLE

ATLANTIC OCEAN

Summer limit of pack ice

Winter limit of pack ice

High bear concentration

Polar bear range

HUDSON BAY

Churchill

UNITED STATES

CANADA

☀ INTRODUCTION

"The beast that walks like man"—that is what Native Americans call the bear. Bears resemble people in so many ways that they have long had special significance to humans. Throughout the Northern Hemisphere, cultures that share the land with any type of bear have always looked upon it with respect and honored it with ceremony.

What makes bears look so much like humans? A bear's tail is so short it hardly shows, and the bear's forward-facing eyes look straight ahead, just like ours. While bears usually travel on all fours, they often stand on their hind legs to get a better view or scent, and they will even walk on their hind legs at times. Most bears, when they stand on their hind legs, are the height of large humans. Some are larger, adding power to their humanlike appearance.

Because of their special significance to people, bears seemed a natural subject for a book featuring the relationships between animals and humans. I chose to focus on polar bears. Finding out how humans have related to polar bears has been difficult. In the past, Eskimo peoples did not have writing, and traveling into the far north to study humans or bears has never been easy. In addition, each group of natives has its own stories and ceremonies, so it is impossible to generalize about these matters.

Eskimo is a word in the Algonquian Indian language, meaning "eaters of raw meat"; it was meant as an insult when used to describe these hardy survivors. Now Eskimo is a general term used to indicate many related northern groups. Some writers prefer to use the word *Inuit,* which is the term used by the Eskimos in most of Canada to describe themselves. It means "the people" in their own language. But other groups have different names for themselves. For convenience, I have used the term Eskimo and have specified the part of the northland where a particular people live.

When I write about animals, I try to visit them in their natural habitats. I was fortunate to be able to go to Churchill, Manitoba, where polar bears gather in the fall, as part of a group organized by the Ursid Research Center of Missoula, Montana. We learned about arctic peoples and ecology, in addition to focusing on polar bears. During my visit to that most southerly habitat of the polar bear and in my research for this book, I have gained great respect for all the living things that find ways of surviving in the harsh northland.

1 THE ICE BEAR

I watch two young bears rear up on their hind legs and lumber toward each other. As they get close, one reaches around the back of the other with a foreleg and pushes him down. Both bears fall onto the snow and begin tussling, much like human youngsters. They look like human wrestlers in slow motion, gently grabbing with paws and teeth.

THE SEAFARING BEAR

The polar bear is the most recent bear to appear on earth, probably during the Ice Age that occurred twenty-five thousand to one hundred thousand years ago. Scientists believe it evolved from the brown bear in the part of the Arctic where Siberia and Alaska come close to each other. Over time, it became superbly adapted to life in the frozen north.

The polar bear (*Ursus maritimus,* meaning "bear of the sea") is the largest of all bears. Females range from 330 to 660 pounds (150 to 300 kilograms). An adult male can weigh a ton and stand ten feet (3 meters) tall on its hind legs. Only an occasional male Kodiak or coastal types of brown bear can match a polar bear in size.

The strength of a polar bear is awesome. One front paw is powerful enough to kill a two-hundred-pound (91-kilogram) ringed seal with one swat. A full-grown male polar bear has nothing to fear, except humans on the hunt or perhaps a bigger, stronger male bear.

Two young bears play fight near Churchill, Manitoba, in Canada.

A polar bear is especially adapted to living on ice and snow. Its furry, slightly webbed feet can be a foot (30.5 centimeters) in diameter. They act like snowshoes when it walks. The thick fur on the feet protects them from the cold and gives them traction on the ice. On land, a polar bear can run twenty-five miles or more per hour (40 kilometers per hour). When it swims, the forefeet act like paddles. The hind feet are held together and used as a rudder for steering.

Polar bear fur keeps the animal extremely warm. The short, thick underfur is densely packed. The longer, coarser guard hairs are hollow, which allows them to trap air and thus insulate the bear's body from the cold, just as do the down feathers in a jacket or quilt. The hollow hairs also trap the warmth of the sun's rays and carry it directly to the bear's black skin, helping to warm the body even when the air temperature is cold. Polar bear fur is not always completely white—it can have a golden hue, with some areas of the coat whiter than others. The bear's color camouflages it on the ice and snow, making it easier for the animal to sneak up on its prey.

LAND OF THE WHITE BEAR

The Arctic is truly the land of the bear—the word *arctic* is derived from the Greek word for bear. Throughout human history, many peoples in the Northern Hemisphere used the northern constellations Ursa Major (Great Bear, also called the Big Dipper) and Ursa Minor (Little Bear, also called the Little Dipper) to guide their travels. An imaginary line drawn from Ursa Major points to the lead star of Ursa Minor. This lead star—the "North Star," or Polaris—indicates the direction of north.

The Arctic contains some of the most extreme living conditions on earth. In regions north of the Arctic Circle, the sun does not rise above the horizon at all during the winter solstice (about December 22). The frozen landscape is lit only by a faint twilight at midday. Traveling farther north, the number of days without the winter sun increases until, arriving at the North Pole, darkness reigns for six months of the year.

Although bears have short tails, the Great and Little Bear constellations have always been drawn with long ones. The bright star in the Little Bear's tail is the North Star.

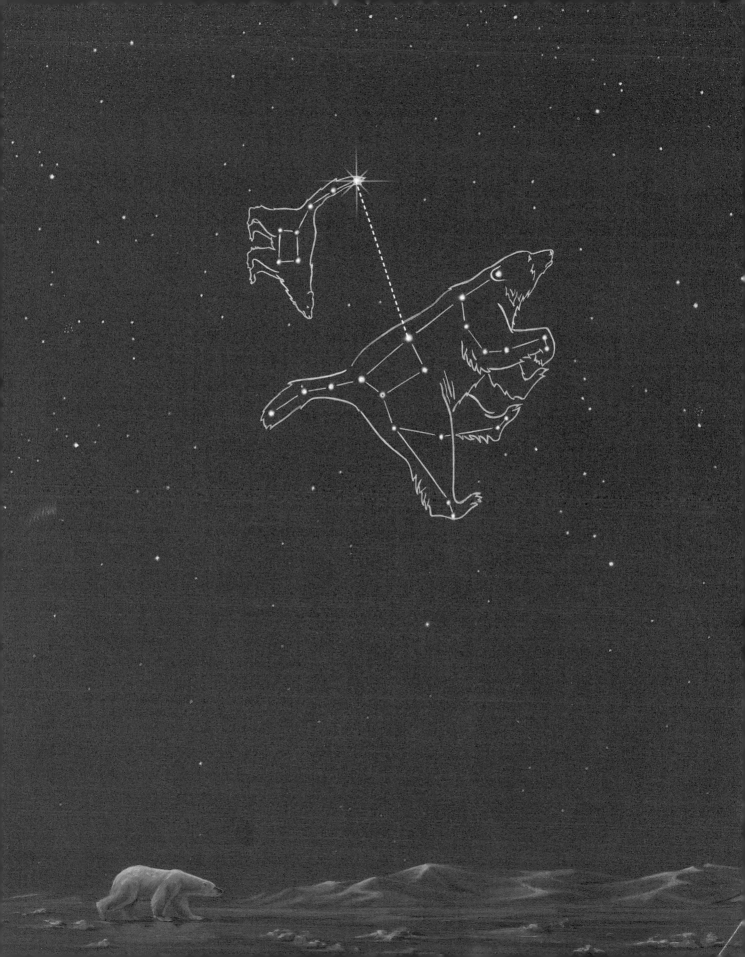

During summer at the North Pole, the sun never sets. Instead of coming up in the east and setting in the west, it moves around above the horizon, providing light twenty-four hours a day.

Even with the perpetual sunlight of summer, however, warmth rarely comes to some arctic regions. In northwest Greenland, in an area about 950 miles (1,520 kilometers) from the North Pole, where the Polar Eskimos live, the average temperature rises above freezing only in July. And ice covers the Arctic Ocean year-round.

Southward, the Arctic blends into the subarctic region below the Arctic Circle.

Although geographers place a line around the globe (the Arctic Circle) and divide these regions, there is no strict division in terms of ecology and weather. The Arctic could be defined by climate—the mean temperature always stays below fifty degrees Fahrenheit (10 degrees Centigrade) in the arctic climate region. This area bulges out south of the Arctic Circle to include the Bering Sea, Hudson and James Bays, as well as southern Greenland. On the other hand, some parts of Alaska, Canada, Scandinavia, and Siberia that fall within the Arctic Circle have a milder climate.

The boundaries of the true Arctic correspond roughly to the tree line, north of which trees do not grow. This treeless expanse is called the tundra. The tundra never thaws completely. Under the surface, at a depth of a few inches to many feet, is a permanent ice layer, called permafrost. The permafrost can be one thousand feet (305 meters) deep. Trees cannot sink their roots into solid ice. In addition, the overlying ground is always wet, because drainage of the moisture from rain or melted snow and ice is blocked by the permafrost. Instead of grass and trees, the tundra is covered

The Arctic is a land of ice and snow, to which the polar bear is perfectly suited. These bears are waiting for the ice to freeze over solidly so they can go seal hunting.

by dwarf shrubs, moss, and lichen, the food of the caribou. This vast land-scape, dotted by shallow lakes and ponds, is characteristic of the Arctic.

While the surface soil layer of the tundra may thaw for a short time during the summer, much of the Arctic is covered with ice and snow year-round. Arctic waters feature two kinds of ice. Land-fast ice is attached to the shore, and pack ice floats on the water. The land-fast ice stays put, but the pack ice can drift long distances.

From January through April, the only open water in the Arctic Ocean consists of "leads," open channels between masses of pack ice pushed this way or that by tidal currents or strong winds. People on pack ice must be ever alert to shifts in the wind or current that could move the ice away from shore, stranding them. The wind and tide can also push huge masses of pack ice together, breaking off chunks that pile up into jagged rows of jumbled ice, called pressure ridges. Pressure ridges can provide high spots from which to survey the surroundings, but they are difficult to cross.

This realm of whiteness, bitter cold, jumbled ice, and frigid waters is the polar bear's home.

2 LIFE OF THE POLAR BEAR

It is only November 1, but already the temperature is close to zero degrees Fahrenheit (−18 degrees Centigrade). From the heated bus that brought me here from the research station in Churchill, I look out at a polar bear lying peacefully on the windswept tundra. It seems untroubled by the freezing cold.

No other creatures are better adapted to the extreme arctic climate. Polar bears can tolerate temperatures below minus fifty degrees Fahrenheit (−46 degrees Centigrade) and swim twenty miles (32 kilometers) in water close to the freezing point.

LONE BEAR OF THE NORTH

Scientists once thought that polar bears were endless wanderers. But they now know that while polar bears do not necessarily remain in a specific area for their entire lives, distinct populations of polar bears live in different arctic regions and rarely mix with one another. The bears north of Siberia and Alaska, where they first evolved from brown bears, look the most like their land-living cousins. Bears living around the island of Spitsbergen are the most different from brown bears. They show the greatest adaptation to an aquatic life, with long necks that make it easier to breathe while swimming and wedge-shaped bodies that can glide smoothly through the water.

The polar bear is one of the world's most solitary creatures. In some

Polar bears in Alaska, like the one above left, are shaped very much like brown bears. Those that live near Spitsbergen, like the one below left, have longer necks and are better shaped for swimming.

areas, there is only one bear for every 104 square miles (269 square kilometers). In a few areas, however, the bears are more concentrated for part of the year. The polar bears living in the mildest climate inhabit Hudson Bay in northern Canada. They spend the winter on the ice, hunting seals, then move to land in summer when the ice melts. The population that spends the summer along the southwestern coast of the bay dens in both summer and winter. In summer, these bears dig dens in the tundra down to the permafrost layer and rest against the ice to keep cool. In fall, they gather along the shore near Churchill to wait for the pack ice to form.

RAISING A FAMILY

In late October or November, while the males hunt on the pack ice, pregnant female polar bears throughout the Arctic stop their wandering and enter

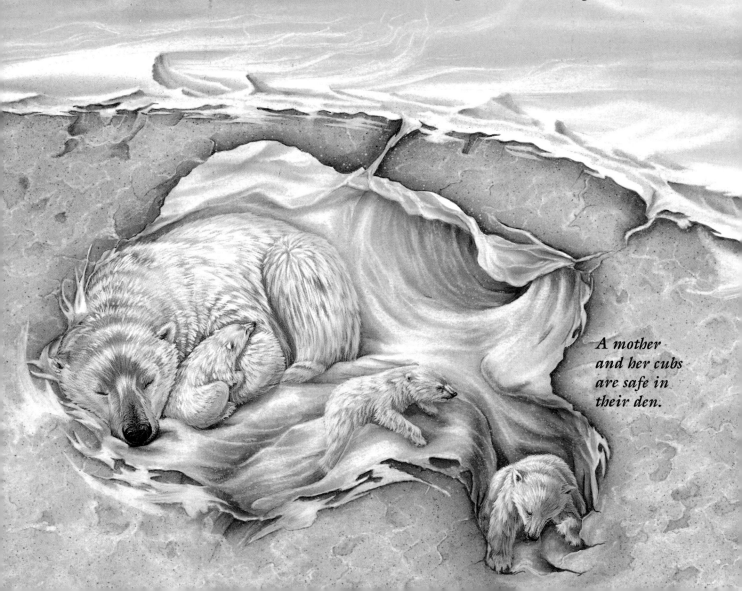

A mother and her cubs are safe in their den.

dens dug into the earth and snow. The den entrance leads into a long tunnel, ending in a rounded chamber, sometimes with additional side rooms or passages. The entrance tunnel penetrates far into the layer of snow covering the protected southwest side of a hill or snowbank, but it is not deep. The ceiling may be only a foot or less from the surface, so some light probably penetrates through the snow.

Some female bears den on land or land-fast ice, but others make their dens on the pack ice. During the time a bear is holed up on pack ice, the ice may drift many miles from where it was when the female entered the den. But polar bears have a good sense of direction, so the female can find her way back to her home area after emerging.

The female stays in the den, quietly and alone, until her one to four cubs are born in January or February. At birth, a polar bear cub is tiny, weighing two pounds (.9 kilogram) or less. Its eyes are closed, and it has only a little fur. In the safety of the den, the infant bear feeds on its mother's rich milk, which contains more than 30 percent fat. (Only seal and whale milk are richer.)

By the time the cub is twenty-six days old, it can hear; and by thirty-three days, its eyes open. At the age of two months, the cub is furry and active, exploring its protected home and playing with its litter mates, if it has any. Meanwhile, its mother remains quiet and sleepy, conserving her energy. If danger threatens, however, she becomes wide awake, ready to protect her cubs from any intruder.

When the family leaves the den in March or April, the cubs are the size of small chubby dogs. Each weighs twenty-two to thirty-three pounds (10 to 15 kilograms). The bears may stay near the den for a couple of weeks while the cubs get used to life in the open; then they head out onto the pack ice together.

During the entire denning period, the mother bear is in a state of hibernation typical of bears. She

doesn't eat, drink, urinate, or defecate. She gets the calories and water she needs from the fat stored in her body. A female polar bear must put on about four hundred pounds (182 kilograms) of fat before entering the den, in order to nourish her cubs while she hibernates. By the time she is able to hunt once more, she has lost about that much weight.

ON THE HUNT

The arctic waters provide abundant food for polar bears. They are especially fond of ringed seals. A hunting polar bear kills a seal about every six days. Normally, the bear eats only the blubber, leaving the meat behind. It may seem strange to us to eat only the fat, but it makes sense for bears. If a bear ate the meat, which is mostly protein, it would have to eat large quantities of snow and ice to get the water necessary to help break down the protein chemically and eliminate the accompanying wastes. Melting that snow and ice and heating it to body temperature would use up about two thousand calories a day. When the bear's body breaks down seal fat, however, water is released in the process. So, by eating only the fat, the bear is not only richly fed, but it also gets enough water to meet its needs.

To hunt, a polar bear may use a number of techniques. Most commonly, it focuses on catching seals at their breathing holes. Seals live underwater, but they must surface periodically to breathe. Every seal has several breathing holes in the ice. When the seal needs to breathe, it comes up through one of the holes, spinning its body around to help keep the hole in the ice open. Over time, the seal's warm breath partially melts the ice and the overlying snow, creating a space between them called an *aglu*. When a polar bear scents an *aglu*, it scrapes away the snow covering it and waits until the seal comes up for air. As the seal surfaces, the bear pins it with a powerful front paw, grabs it with its teeth, and pulls it onto the ice with bone-breaking force.

While seals, especially ringed seals, are their most important food, polar bears also feed on the carcasses of beached whales, as well as small land mammals, seabirds, and even plants. The more southern bears, which live on ice-free land during the warmer months, eat berries during summer and fall. They may also forage in the kelp for mussels at low tide.

GROWING UP

Polar bear cubs learn how to hunt from their mother. She may even use them to make her job easier. The mother bear will wait by one of the seal's breathing holes after stationing her cubs at nearby holes. The cubs' presence makes an alert seal retreat rather than come to the surface to breathe. The seal is eventually forced to the surface at the hole where the mother quietly waits.

The young usually stay with their mother for two to two and a half years. After that, they are on their own. In the meantime, the female mates (between March and June) and gives birth to new cubs six and a half to nine months later, once her previous cubs are independent.

Polar bears are ready to mate when they are five or six years old and weigh 330 to 660 pounds (150 to 300 kilograms). Males may not reach their full adult weight, however, until they are ten or eleven.

In the wild, polar bears that survive their early years may live to be thirty. Captive bears often live even longer.

Polar bear cubs can help in the hunt by staying near a seal breathing hole. Seeing them there, the seal is forced to get air at another hole nearby, where their mother waits patiently.

3 THE ICE BEAR'S PEOPLE

The people commonly called Eskimos, who inhabit the Arctic, arrived in the New World thousands of years after the original inhabitants of North America. The Eskimo ancestors traveled from Siberia in boats or by foot across the arctic ice. They came in waves of migration, starting about five thousand years ago and ending around three thousand years ago.

ARCTIC IMMIGRANTS

The earliest arctic settlers had made it all the way east to Greenland by around 2000 B.C. About a thousand years later, that early culture merged with that of more recent migrants into what archaeologists call the Dorset culture. Many Dorset artifacts survive to this day, including beautifully carved ivory images of animals, such as polar bears and falcons. Dorset culture was overwhelmed by later migrations of Eskimo peoples who possessed advanced technology. These later peoples used dogs to pull sleds across the snow and ice. They built skin-covered boats from which they hunted sea mammals with deadly harpoons. By A.D. 1300, the Dorset culture had just about disappeared.

ESKIMOS OF THE ARCTIC

After arriving in North America, the Eskimos colonized a vast area extending all the way from western Alaska across the Canadian Arctic to Greenland.

Life in the Arctic is very hard, but the Eskimos learned how to survive there.

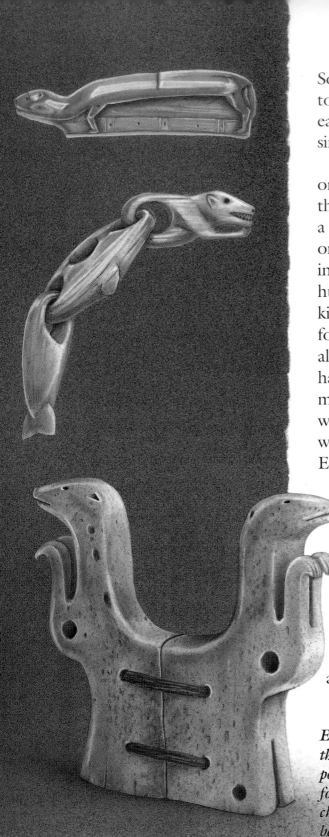

Some of them remained in Siberia and live there to this day. While many Eskimo groups exist, each with its own unique way of life, all share similar languages and cultural traditions.

In the past, living in the Arctic meant depending on wildlife for survival, for farming was out of the question. Wild plants were available only for a short time during the year, and the Eskimos' only domesticated animal was the dog. So finding food meant finding animals that could be hunted. Any fish or mammal the Eskimos could kill provided vital food and other useful materials for the village. Traditionally, Eskimos respected all living things and believed that every creature had a soul. But they also believed that if an animal was killed properly and its body was treated with respect, the animal's soul would cooperate with further hunting. For example, the Netsilik Eskimos believed that if all the rituals associated with the killing of a seal were observed, the seal's soul would be pleased and would be reincarnated into another seal's body. That seal would then allow itself to be killed by the same hunter who had shown himself to be so respectful. As one hunter put it, "We live by killing souls."

Most Eskimo peoples historically lived along the sea, the most reliable source of arctic game: fish, seals, walruses, and whales.

Eskimos decorated their tools with animal images. At the top is an ivory knife handle in the likeness of a polar bear. In the middle, the gracefully carved handle for a drag line illustrates the belief that animals can change form; it shows a feared beast that is half polar bear, half whale. At the bottom, polar bears adorn a harpoon rest made from walrus jawbone.

Sea mammals provided not only meat but also hides for clothing, housing, and boat building; oil for cooking and lighting; and ivory and bone for toolmaking and art. To this day, many Eskimos retain aspects of traditional life.

Land mammals, especially caribou, could also be important sources of food and materials. One group in Canada, the Caribou Eskimo, lived inland and once depended on the caribou for their survival. Mountain sheep, musk-oxen, foxes, wolves, and other animals also provided meat and/or fur.

But by far the most challenging and dangerous arctic land animal to hunt is the polar bear, which Eskimos call Nanook.

HUNTING NANOOK

Before Europeans introduced the rifle, native hunters had to stand their ground against the great bear, using only harpoons and knives and the help of their sled dogs to distract the prey. When a bear was sighted, a traveling Eskimo would excitedly turn his sled to pursue it. Early in this century, when anthropologist Knud Rasmussen asked an old Greenland Eskimo what was the greatest happiness, the man answered, "To run across fresh bear tracks and be ahead of all the other sledges."

On the far right is a harpoon, with its detachable head. Top left shows another view of the head. It is beautifully carved with special decorations because Eskimo hunters believed that sea mammals became angry if they were attacked by ugly weapons. At bottom left is a knife made from stone.

When the hunter got close to the bear, he would cut his dogs loose from the sled. The dogs would run after the bear, surround it, and harass it by biting at its rear end, expertly dodging the bear's angry swats. While the bear was held at bay by the dogs, the hunter would lash his special bear-killing blade onto his harpoon. The blade used in bear hunting was much longer than the one used for seal hunts. Then the hunter approached the bear cautiously, waiting for a chance to plunge the harpoon into the big animal's neck.

Sometimes the hunter's dogs would smell a denned bear. Then the hunter would use his harpoon to poke through the snow until he found the den by feeling either that the harpoon had encountered an air space or, more dangerously, that it had poked the bear itself. A hunter could be in big trouble if the bear bit and broke the shaft of his harpoon!

Eskimo dogs attack a polar bear by biting at its rear end. When the bear turns around to face the dog behind him, the others can attack.

Hunting polar bears was very dangerous. The bear could kill the hunter easily with one swat of its huge, powerful front paw or one bite from its big, sharp teeth. Many Eskimo men had scars to remind them of their encounters with polar bears. But partly because of the great danger, successfully hunting a polar bear brought honor and respect. Men relished the opportunity to gain prestige and to acquire a useful and beautiful hide, as well as to share meat with the village.

The old Eskimo way of life, described as "a long walk on an empty stomach," has now given way to modern comforts and conveniences for most Eskimos. While only some traditions survive, a respect for the great white bear remains. To this day, among Eskimos in northwest Greenland, a young man gains respect as an adult by successfully hunting a polar bear and thus obtaining his own pair of polar bear pants.

4 MEANINGS OF THE BEAR

As I enter the Eskimo Museum in Churchill, Manitoba, I am amazed at the variety of beautiful ivory and stone carvings that depict native life. In a case near the door is a carving by a native artist that tells a story: A man bends over a seal hole and is surprised by a polar bear that knocks him down. The man's two dogs attack the bear, which then turns on them, and the man kills the bear with his knife. As it dies, the bear changes into the man's mother-in-law. She had taken on the form of a bear to frighten him, and he has killed the bear without realizing who it really was.

ANIMALS AND PEOPLE

In the Eskimo world, as in many other societies, the dividing line between humans and animals was often blurred. People felt that they could take the form of animals, and that animals could just as easily disguise themselves as humans.

Throughout the Northern Hemisphere, where most of the world's bears live, native societies have tales in which bears take on human form. One especially common story is that of the woman who married a bear. In the usual telling of this tale, a young woman goes out to gather food, such as berries, and encounters a bear. At first she is frightened, but the bear tells

The shaman is a powerful person in many traditional societies, including that of the Eskimos. A shaman is believed to leave his body and fly through the air (as shown symbolically above the singing shaman at left) or swim through the water to visit deities or retrieve lost souls.

her not to be afraid, and they talk together. He takes her to his home, where he removes his bearskin to reveal that he is really a man. He lives in a village of similar bear people. The girl marries the bear man and is sworn to secrecy about his true nature. But eventually she meets up with one of her brothers, who wants to know where she has been. She can't resist telling him the truth, breaking her promise to her husband. This break in trust leads to tragedy. In some versions, the bear kills his wife for betraying him, and in others her brothers kill him. The girl has learned important secrets of finding food or medicinal herbs from the bear, or he has revealed important rituals to her. She passes these on to her people.

Other Eskimo stories tell of people raising polar bear children, or bears raising human offspring.

THE BEAR AS A HELPING SPIRIT

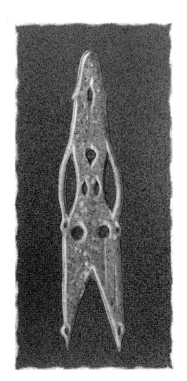

This Dorset carving of a man-bear shows the similarity of polar bear and human.

Many native cultures believed that humans could communicate with animal spirits if they used the right techniques. Much could be learned through such communication, and often it was considered critically important to the survival of the tribe. Relationships between the Eskimos and animals were especially crucial, since these people depended entirely on hunting for their survival.

The shaman was the person who mediated between the material and spiritual worlds, and animals were thought to be helping spirits that made the contact or provided vital information. Perhaps because the bear seems so much like a person, or because it is so powerful, it was the greatest helping spirit of all to many native peoples. The bear gave a shaman power and guidance and provided him with other helping spirits.

The polar bear's spiritual power has been valued since ancient times. Many carved ivory images of polar bears in a standing posture—when they look most like humans— have been found from the Dorset culture. Most of the bear figurines have an open mouth, a symbol of the connection of the breath with the soul.

These carved figures were probably connected with the

shaman's spirit journey, his visit to the world of spirits, where he could get help for his people when they were in trouble. The bear spirit could carry the shaman to the moon or into the sea, where he went to get help from Sedna, the most powerful of the sea-dwelling spirits. The bear spirit could also protect the shaman from evil.

As an Eskimo from Baffin Island told anthropologist Franz Boas in 1883, if a shaman wanted the bear spirit to be his helper, he had to risk his life by making direct contact with the animals themselves. He had to go out alone to the edge of the land-fast ice and call to the bears. The bears would come, the Eskimo said, a big group of them, frightening the shaman terribly. If the shaman fell over backward in his fright, he would die immediately. But if he landed on his face, one of the bears would step forward and offer himself. The story then goes that on the way back to the shaman's home, the bear would catch a seal for his new master. From then on, the man would be a great shaman who could count on his bear for help when he needed it.

Eskimos believed that the powerful bear could also be used by a

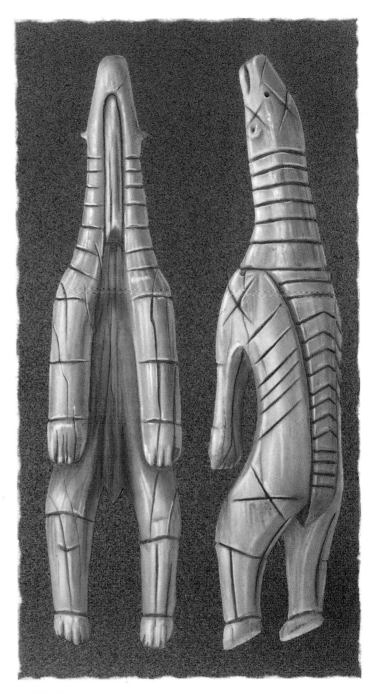

This ivory polar bear was also made by the Dorset people. The cavity in the neck, covered by a sliding lid, held red ocher powder, which the Eskimos used during ceremonies.

bad shaman for evil ends. Legends tell of shamans who used their bear spirit to kill people. But such a negative bear spirit could become angry and get out of control, killing its master.

AFTER THE HUNT

Because the polar bear was so powerful, both physically and spiritually, great care had to be taken to show respect after a successful bear hunt. The hunters feared that, if they did not honor the soul of the dead bear properly, it could turn into a bloodthirsty monster or keep the village from ever killing another bear.

A Jesuit missionary, Bellarmine Lafortune, recorded details of bear hunts among the King Island Eskimos of Alaska during the 1930s. After the hunter returned with the dead bear, the skull was placed on a raised bench in the communal house. The people brought gifts and placed them near the skull. If the bear was male, a drill or carving knife might be left; needle cases and skin scrapers were appropriate gifts for a female bear. The gifts became the property of the bear's soul.

The rituals that followed a successful hunt went on for days. If the bear was a male, the hunter had to feed the community for four days with traditional dishes such as snow with seal oil and berries. For a female bear, the feasting lasted five days. Finally, a polar bear dance was held. The skull was then taken out on the moving ice, where the bear's spirit was released.

The Netsilik Eskimos of the Canadian Arctic believed that the bear's soul remained on the tip of the hunter's spear for several days after the hunt. To keep the bear's soul from becoming an evil spirit, work in the village had to cease, and the bear's skin was brought inside the house. Gifts to the bear's soul were placed on the skin. Only after the soul departed could normal village life be resumed.

Most Eskimos today have become Christians. But they still respect the intelligence and power of the polar bear. They believe it is bad luck to joke about bears or to show disrespect in any way.

Native peoples have great respect for bears. Here, an Eskimo makes an offering to the spirit of a bear he hunted successfully.

5 PEOPLE & POLAR BEARS TODAY

As I sit in the bus, I see the rest of my group hurrying down the gravel road. One of them yells, "There's a bear out here!" I look, and there it is, a golden white polar bear, walking fast behind the people hurrying to get back on the bus.

The bear shows no fear. It comes up to the bus as the passengers hastily raise their windows. The bear saunters along the side, putting its paws up here and there to peer at the two-leggeds inside. Finally, it wanders slowly off across the tundra, its coat gleaming in the sunlight.

THE CHURCHILL PROBLEM

Every October, the gathering of polar bears along the western shores of Hudson Bay presents a problem for people living in Churchill. The bears are not hunted, and many of them have no fear of humans. The bears have come from their summer denning sites to wait for the pack ice to form on Hudson Bay so they can go out to hunt for seals. The urge to go out on the ice is strong. Sometimes they arrive weeks before the bay freezes over.

The biggest males, which can chase off smaller bears, tend to gather on Cape Churchill, where the pack ice forms first. During the fall, bears often wander through town in their attempts to reach the cape. If they appear during daylight hours, they can get in trouble with people.

Human residents of Churchill must be very careful at this time. A surprised or cornered bear can attack. Once a woman left a pie to cool on a

At Churchill, people can get a close look at polar bears in late October.

windowsill during late October. A polar bear was attracted by the scent and entered the house. The only way to get rid of the bear was to kill it.

Officials do their best to help people avoid such tragic encounters. They give talks to schoolchildren and local groups about keeping garbage indoors and watching where they walk to make sure bears are not around. If someone sees a bear in town, people are alerted so they can avoid the animal. Fortunately, most polar bears live far away from human settlements, so they don't pose a danger to people—or vice versa.

This mother and her cubs were trapped because they wandered too close to town. Now that the pack ice has formed, they are being released to go out on the ice.

DANGER
BEAR
TRAP

SURVIVAL OF THE WHITE BEAR

Thirty years ago, polar bears were hunted, without much regulation, for their beautiful fur and their meat. Scientists began to worry about the white bear's survival, and in 1973 the five polar bear nations—the United States, Canada, Norway (for the Svalbard Islands, which include Spitsbergen), Denmark (for Greenland), and the former USSR (for Siberia)—met to determine how to save the polar bear.

Their plans, which help regulate hunting and encourage research, have proven very successful. The number of polar bears has increased. Now there are between twenty thousand and thirty thousand across the Arctic.

Few people brave the polar bear's cold and icy realm, so, with restrictions on hunting, it is left largely to live as it always has—hunting seals, having cubs, and surviving in its harsh environment. The polar bear is protected in the United States by the Marine Mammal Protection Act, which bars hunting except for native subsistence. Only resident natives can hunt bears in Greenland as well. In Spitsbergen, polar bear hunting is completely prohibited. Russia officially bans polar bear hunting. In Canada, each Eskimo village receives a number of permits to hunt polar bears each year. The village keeps a few permits for its young men to prove their bravery and sells the rest to non-native hunters who can afford the $10,000 price tag.

Despite the present healthy condition of polar bear populations, the danger of human intrusion is ever present. Since the breakup of the Soviet Union, no one knows for sure what is happening with Russia's polar bears, but almost certainly there is increased poaching. The country has severe economic problems, and enforcing wildlife protection laws, especially in

remote areas, is a low priority for a government struggling to survive.

A further threat to polar bears is the pressure to allow extraction of oil and gas from the Arctic. Since many bears den in areas where there are oil and gas reserves, such as in the Arctic National Wildlife Refuge, human activity in those places could be disastrous to polar bear reproduction.

Despite its remoteness, the Arctic is also plagued by pollution. Dangerous chemicals such as PCBs can travel long distances, carried by wind or water. In Norway's Svalbard Islands, for example, converging air and water currents from the United States, Europe, and Russia have resulted in

elevated PCB levels in polar bears that live there. No one can be sure how these chemicals might affect the bears. Another threat is global warming, which could melt the ice that polar bears depend on in their hunting.

If we do the things necessary to protect the polar bear, we will also be preserving the arctic environment for all its other creatures. By showing respect for the bear, as the Eskimos do, we value a vast ecosystem, one that tests its residents with some of the most difficult conditions for life. That creatures such as polar bears can live comfortably there teaches us about the adaptability of living things to some of nature's greatest challenges.

INDEX